Test Colors

Test Colors

Test Colors

Test Colors

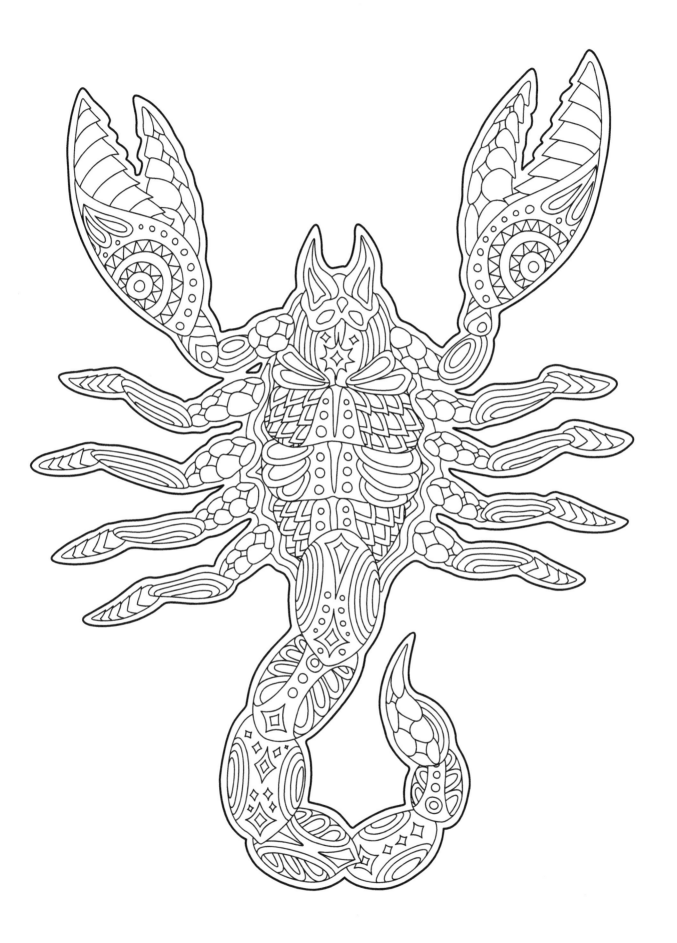

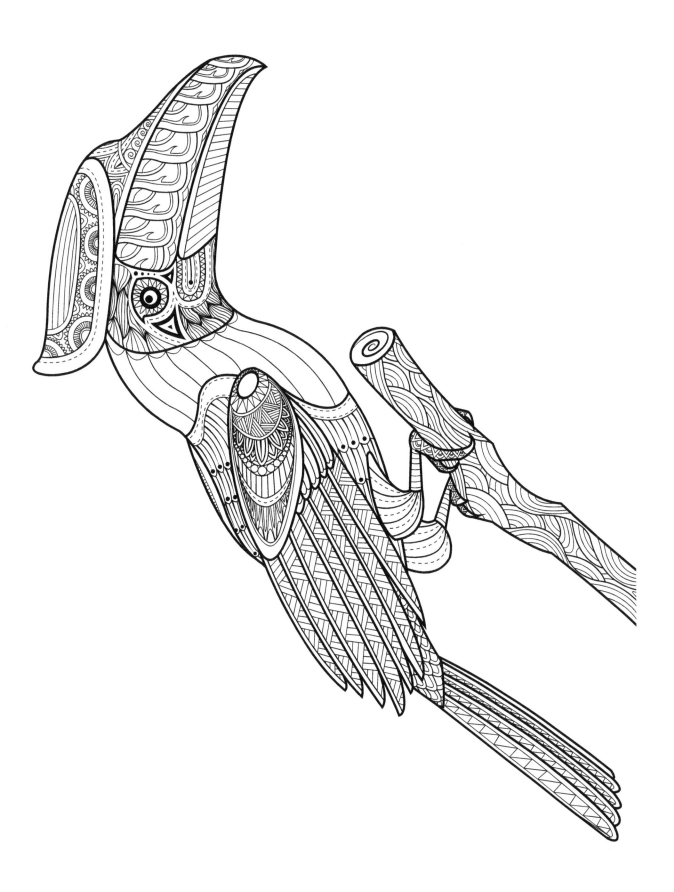

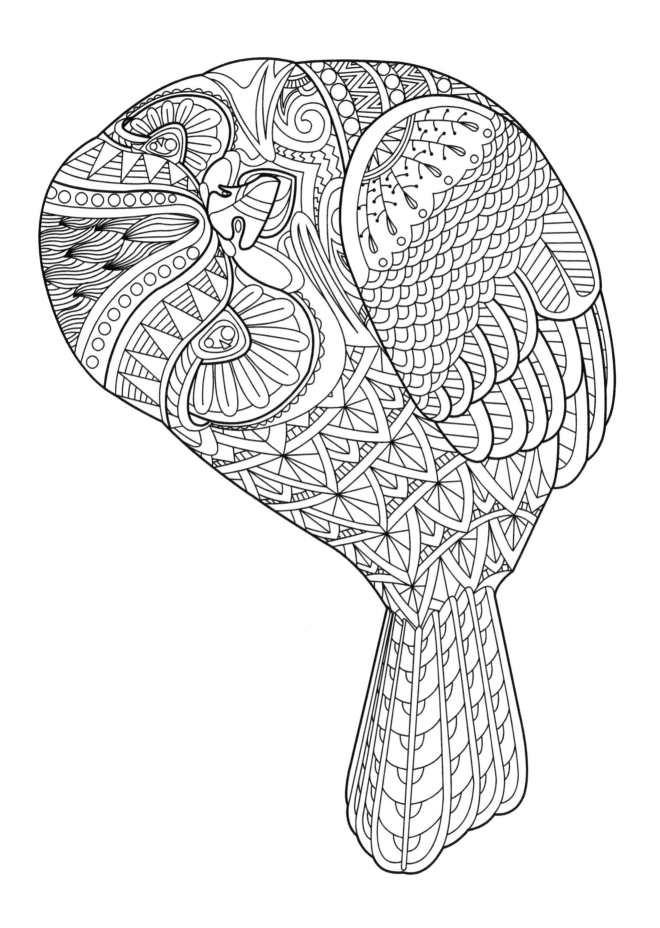

Test Colors

Test Colors

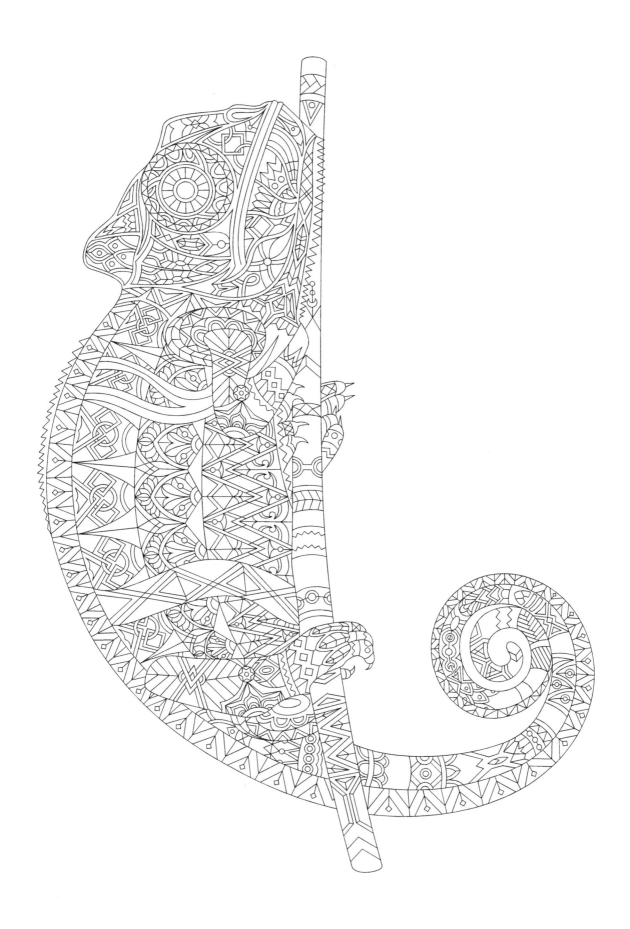

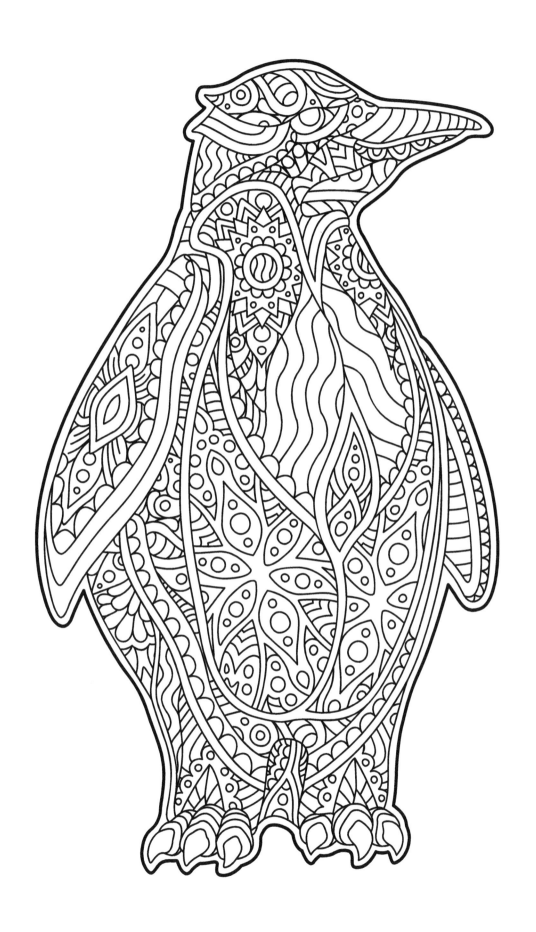

Test Colors

Test Colors

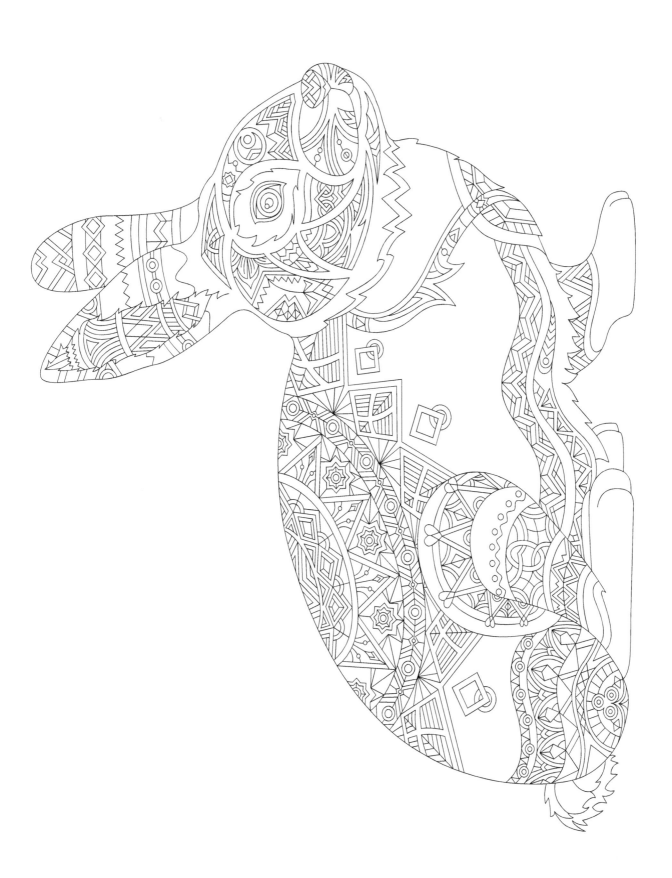

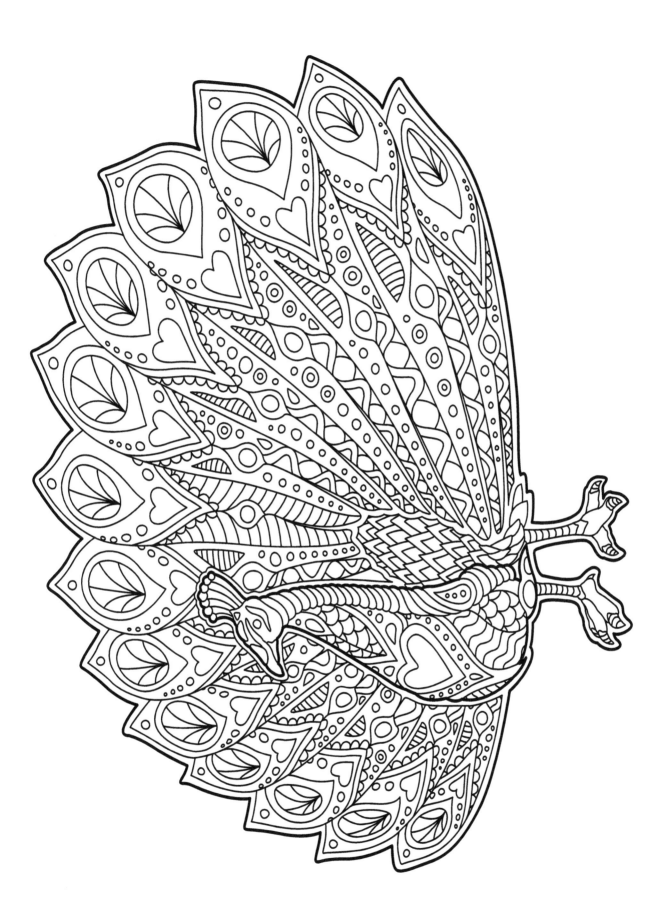

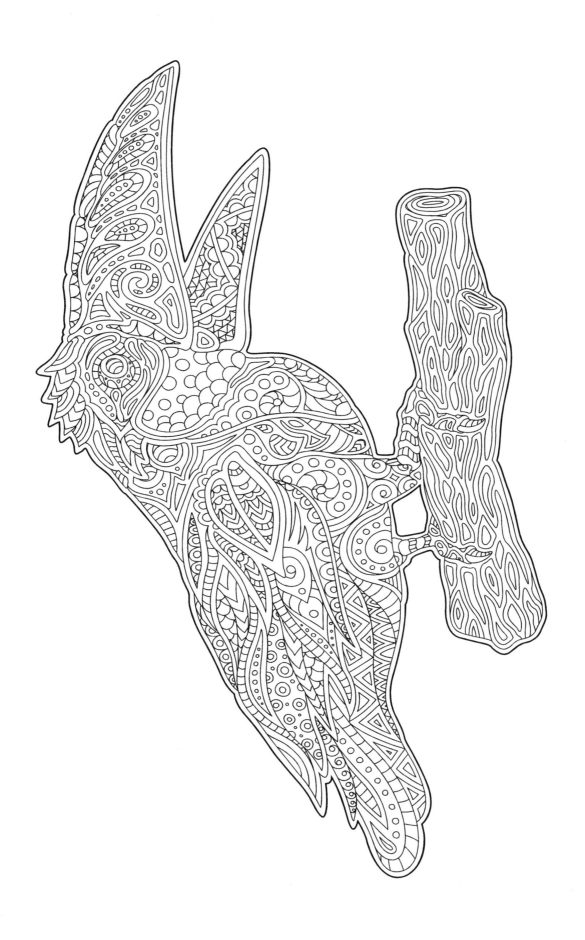

CPSIA information can be obtained
at www.ICGtesting.com
Printed in the USA
BVHW011017101021
618624BV00024B/749